Beer Brewing
Journal

Beer name:

Beer Style:

Brewer:

Date brewed:

Brewing method:

Boil size		Target OG	
Batch size		Target FG	

Actual OG		Target ABV	
Actual FG		Actual ABV	

GRAINS		HOPS		TOTAL IBU	
Name	Amount	Name	Amount	Time	IBU

YEAST		OTHER ADDITIONS	
Name			
Type			
Style			

MASH AND SPARGE SCHEDULE

Time	Temp	✓	

BOIL SCHEDULE

Time	✓	

FERMENTATION LOG

Date	Activity

Beer name:

Beer Style:

Brewer:

Date brewed:

Brewing method:

Boil size	
Batch size	

Target OG	
Target FG	

Actual OG	
Actual FG	

Target ABV	
Actual ABV	

GRAINS	
Name	Amount

HOPS		TOTAL IBU	
Name	Amount	Time	IBU

YEAST	
Name	
Type	
Style	

OTHER ADDITIONS	

MASH AND SPARGE SCHEDULE

Time	Temp	✓	

BOIL SCHEDULE

Time	✓	

FERMENTATION LOG

Date	Activity

Beer name:	

Beer Style:	

Brewer:	

Date brewed:	

Brewing method:	

Boil size		Target OG	
Batch size		Target FG	

Actual OG		Target ABV	
Actual FG		Actual ABV	

GRAINS		HOPS		TOTAL IBU	
Name	Amount	Name	Amount	Time	IBU

YEAST		OTHER ADDITIONS	
Name			
Type			
Style			

MASH AND SPARGE SCHEDULE

Time	Temp	✓	

BOIL SCHEDULE

Time	✓	

FERMENTATION LOG

Date	Activity

Beer name:

Beer Style:

Brewer:

Date brewed:

Brewing method:

Boil size	
Batch size	

Target OG	
Target FG	

Actual OG	
Actual FG	

Target ABV	
Actual ABV	

GRAINS	
Name	Amount

HOPS		TOTAL IBU	
Name	Amount	Time	IBU

YEAST	
Name	
Type	
Style	

OTHER ADDITIONS	

MASH AND SPARGE SCHEDULE

Time	Temp	✓	

BOIL SCHEDULE

Time	✓	

FERMENTATION LOG

Date	Activity

Beer name:

Beer Style:

Brewer:

Date brewed:

Brewing method:

Boil size	
Batch size	

Target OG	
Target FG	

Actual OG	
Actual FG	

Target ABV	
Actual ABV	

GRAINS			HOPS		TOTAL IBU	
Name	Amount		Name	Amount	Time	IBU

YEAST		OTHER ADDITIONS	
Name			
Type			
Style			

MASH AND SPARGE SCHEDULE

Time	Temp	✓	

BOIL SCHEDULE

Time	✓	

FERMENTATION LOG

Date	Activity

Beer name:

Beer Style:

Brewer:

Date brewed:

Brewing method:

Boil size	
Batch size	

Target OG	
Target FG	

Actual OG	
Actual FG	

Target ABV	
Actual ABV	

GRAINS	
Name	Amount

HOPS		TOTAL IBU	
Name	Amount	Time	IBU

YEAST	
Name	
Type	
Style	

OTHER ADDITIONS	

MASH AND SPARGE SCHEDULE

Time	Temp	✓	

BOIL SCHEDULE

Time	✓	

FERMENTATION LOG

Date	Activity

Beer name:	

Beer Style:	

Brewer:	

Date brewed:	

Brewing method:	

Boil size	
Batch size	

Target OG	
Target FG	

Actual OG	
Actual FG	

Target ABV	
Actual ABV	

GRAINS		HOPS		TOTAL IBU	
Name	Amount	Name	Amount	Time	IBU

YEAST		OTHER ADDITIONS	
Name			
Type			
Style			

MASH AND SPARGE SCHEDULE

Time	Temp	✓	

BOIL SCHEDULE

Time	✓	

FERMENTATION LOG

Date	Activity

Beer name:

Beer Style:

Brewer:

Date brewed:

Brewing method:

Boil size	
Batch size	

Target OG	
Target FG	

Actual OG	
Actual FG	

Target ABV	
Actual ABV	

GRAINS		HOPS		TOTAL IBU	
Name	Amount	Name	Amount	Time	IBU

YEAST		OTHER ADDITIONS	
Name			
Type			
Style			

MASH AND SPARGE SCHEDULE

Time	Temp	✓	

BOIL SCHEDULE

Time	✓	

FERMENTATION LOG

Date	Activity

Beer name:	

Beer Style:	

Brewer:	

Date brewed:	

Brewing method:	

Boil size	
Batch size	

Target OG	
Target FG	

Actual OG	
Actual FG	

Target ABV	
Actual ABV	

GRAINS			HOPS		TOTAL IBU	
Name	Amount		Name	Amount	Time	IBU

YEAST		OTHER ADDITIONS	
Name			
Type			
Style			

MASH AND SPARGE SCHEDULE

Time	Temp	✓	

BOIL SCHEDULE

Time	✓	

FERMENTATION LOG

Date	Activity

Beer name:

Beer Style:

Brewer:

Date brewed:

Brewing method:

Boil size	
Batch size	

Target OG	
Target FG	

Actual OG	
Actual FG	

Target ABV	
Actual ABV	

GRAINS	
Name	Amount

HOPS		TOTAL IBU	
Name	Amount	Time	IBU

YEAST	
Name	
Type	
Style	

OTHER ADDITIONS	

MASH AND SPARGE SCHEDULE

Time	Temp	✓	

BOIL SCHEDULE

Time	✓	

FERMENTATION LOG

Date	Activity

Beer name:

Beer Style:

Brewer:

Date brewed:

Brewing method:

Boil size	
Batch size	

Actual OG	
Actual FG	

Target OG	
Target FG	

Target ABV	
Actual ABV	

GRAINS	
Name	Amount

HOPS		TOTAL IBU	
Name	Amount	Time	IBU

YEAST	
Name	
Type	
Style	

OTHER ADDITIONS	

MASH AND SPARGE SCHEDULE

Time	Temp	✓	

BOIL SCHEDULE

Time	✓	

FERMENTATION LOG

Date	Activity

Beer name:

Beer Style:

Brewer:

Date brewed:

Brewing method:

Boil size	
Batch size	

Target OG	
Target FG	

Actual OG	
Actual FG	

Target ABV	
Actual ABV	

GRAINS

Name	Amount

HOPS | TOTAL IBU

Name	Amount	Time	IBU

YEAST

Name	
Type	
Style	

OTHER ADDITIONS

MASH AND SPARGE SCHEDULE

Time	Temp	✓	

BOIL SCHEDULE

Time	✓	

FERMENTATION LOG

Date	Activity

Beer name:

Beer Style:

Brewer:

Date brewed:

Brewing method:

Boil size	
Batch size	

Target OG	
Target FG	

Actual OG	
Actual FG	

Target ABV	
Actual ABV	

GRAINS		HOPS		TOTAL IBU	
Name	Amount	Name	Amount	Time	IBU

YEAST		OTHER ADDITIONS	
Name			
Type			
Style			

MASH AND SPARGE SCHEDULE

Time	Temp	✓	

BOIL SCHEDULE

Time	✓	

FERMENTATION LOG

Date	Activity

Beer name:

Beer Style:

Brewer:

Date brewed:

Brewing method:

Boil size	
Batch size	

Target OG	
Target FG	

Actual OG	
Actual FG	

Target ABV	
Actual ABV	

GRAINS	
Name	Amount

HOPS		TOTAL IBU	
Name	Amount	Time	IBU

YEAST	
Name	
Type	
Style	

OTHER ADDITIONS	

MASH AND SPARGE SCHEDULE

Time	Temp	✓	

BOIL SCHEDULE

Time	✓	

FERMENTATION LOG

Date	Activity

Beer name:

Beer Style:

Brewer:

Date brewed:

Brewing method:

Boil size	
Batch size	

Target OG	
Target FG	

Actual OG	
Actual FG	

Target ABV	
Actual ABV	

GRAINS	
Name	Amount

HOPS		TOTAL IBU	
Name	Amount	Time	IBU

YEAST	
Name	
Type	
Style	

OTHER ADDITIONS	

MASH AND SPARGE SCHEDULE

Time	Temp	✓	

BOIL SCHEDULE

Time	✓	

FERMENTATION LOG

Date	Activity

Beer name:

Beer Style:

Brewer:

Date brewed:

Brewing method:

Boil size	
Batch size	

Target OG	
Target FG	

Actual OG	
Actual FG	

Target ABV	
Actual ABV	

GRAINS			HOPS			TOTAL IBU	
Name	Amount		Name	Amount	Time	IBU

YEAST	
Name	
Type	
Style	

OTHER ADDITIONS	

MASH AND SPARGE SCHEDULE

Time	Temp	✓	

BOIL SCHEDULE

Time	✓	

FERMENTATION LOG

Date	Activity

Beer name:

Beer Style:

Brewer:

Date brewed:

Brewing method:

Boil size	
Batch size	

Target OG	
Target FG	

Actual OG	
Actual FG	

Target ABV	
Actual ABV	

GRAINS			HOPS		TOTAL IBU	
Name	Amount		Name	Amount	Time	IBU

YEAST	
Name	
Type	
Style	

OTHER ADDITIONS	

MASH AND SPARGE SCHEDULE

Time	Temp	✓	

BOIL SCHEDULE

Time	✓	

FERMENTATION LOG

Date	Activity

Beer name:

Beer Style:

Brewer:

Date brewed:

Brewing method:

Boil size	
Batch size	

Target OG	
Target FG	

Actual OG	
Actual FG	

Target ABV	
Actual ABV	

GRAINS

Name	Amount

HOPS | TOTAL IBU

Name	Amount	Time	IBU

YEAST

Name	
Type	
Style	

OTHER ADDITIONS

MASH AND SPARGE SCHEDULE

Time	Temp	✓	

BOIL SCHEDULE

Time	✓	

FERMENTATION LOG

Date	Activity

Beer name:

Beer Style:

Brewer:

Date brewed:

Brewing method:

Boil size	
Batch size	

Target OG	
Target FG	

Actual OG	
Actual FG	

Target ABV	
Actual ABV	

GRAINS		HOPS		TOTAL IBU	
Name	Amount	Name	Amount	Time	IBU

YEAST		OTHER ADDITIONS	
Name			
Type			
Style			

MASH AND SPARGE SCHEDULE

Time	Temp	✓	

BOIL SCHEDULE

Time	✓	

FERMENTATION LOG

Date	Activity

Beer name:

Beer Style:

Brewer:

Date brewed:

Brewing method:

Boil size	
Batch size	

Target OG	
Target FG	

Actual OG	
Actual FG	

Target ABV	
Actual ABV	

GRAINS	
Name	Amount

HOPS		TOTAL IBU	
Name	Amount	Time	IBU

YEAST	
Name	
Type	
Style	

OTHER ADDITIONS	

MASH AND SPARGE SCHEDULE

Time	Temp	✓	

BOIL SCHEDULE

Time	✓	

FERMENTATION LOG

Date	Activity

Beer name:	

Beer Style:	

Brewer:	

Date brewed:	

Brewing method:	

Boil size	
Batch size	

Target OG	
Target FG	

Actual OG	
Actual FG	

Target ABV	
Actual ABV	

GRAINS

Name	Amount

HOPS / TOTAL IBU

Name	Amount	Time	IBU

YEAST

Name	
Type	
Style	

OTHER ADDITIONS

MASH AND SPARGE SCHEDULE

Time	Temp	✓	

BOIL SCHEDULE

Time	✓	

FERMENTATION LOG

Date	Activity

Beer name:

Beer Style:

Brewer:

Date brewed:

Brewing method:

Boil size	
Batch size	

Target OG	
Target FG	

Actual OG	
Actual FG	

Target ABV	
Actual ABV	

GRAINS		HOPS		TOTAL IBU	
Name	Amount	Name	Amount	Time	IBU

YEAST		OTHER ADDITIONS	
Name			
Type			
Style			

MASH AND SPARGE SCHEDULE

Time	Temp	✓	

BOIL SCHEDULE

Time	✓	

FERMENTATION LOG

Date	Activity

Beer name:

Beer Style:

Brewer:

Date brewed:

Brewing method:

Boil size	
Batch size	

Actual OG	
Actual FG	

Target OG	
Target FG	

Target ABV	
Actual ABV	

GRAINS	
Name	Amount

HOPS		TOTAL IBU	
Name	Amount	Time	IBU

YEAST	
Name	
Type	
Style	

OTHER ADDITIONS	

MASH AND SPARGE SCHEDULE

Time	Temp	✓	

BOIL SCHEDULE

Time	✓	

FERMENTATION LOG

Date	Activity

Beer name:	

Beer Style:	

Brewer:	

Date brewed:	

Brewing method:	

Boil size	
Batch size	

Target OG	
Target FG	

Actual OG	
Actual FG	

Target ABV	
Actual ABV	

GRAINS		HOPS		TOTAL IBU	
Name	Amount	Name	Amount	Time	IBU

YEAST		OTHER ADDITIONS	
Name			
Type			
Style			

MASH AND SPARGE SCHEDULE

Time	Temp	✓	

BOIL SCHEDULE

Time	✓	

FERMENTATION LOG

Date	Activity

Beer name:	

Beer Style:	

Brewer:	

Date brewed:	

Brewing method:	

Boil size	
Batch size	

Actual OG	
Actual FG	

Target OG	
Target FG	

Target ABV	
Actual ABV	

GRAINS	
Name	Amount

HOPS		TOTAL IBU	
Name	Amount	Time	IBU

YEAST	
Name	
Type	
Style	

OTHER ADDITIONS	

MASH AND SPARGE SCHEDULE

Time	Temp	✓	

BOIL SCHEDULE

Time	✓	

FERMENTATION LOG

Date	Activity

Beer name:

Beer Style:

Brewer:

Date brewed:

Brewing method:

Boil size	
Batch size	

Target OG	
Target FG	

Actual OG	
Actual FG	

Target ABV	
Actual ABV	

GRAINS		
Name	Amount

HOPS		TOTAL IBU	
Name	Amount	Time	IBU

YEAST	
Name	
Type	
Style	

OTHER ADDITIONS	

MASH AND SPARGE SCHEDULE

Time	Temp	✓	

BOIL SCHEDULE

Time	✓	

FERMENTATION LOG

Date	Activity

Beer name:	

Beer Style:	

Brewer:	

Date brewed:	

Brewing method:	

Boil size		Target OG	
Batch size		Target FG	

Actual OG		Target ABV	
Actual FG		Actual ABV	

GRAINS		HOPS		TOTAL IBU	
Name	Amount	Name	Amount	Time	IBU

YEAST		OTHER ADDITIONS	
Name			
Type			
Style			

MASH AND SPARGE SCHEDULE

Time	Temp	✓	

BOIL SCHEDULE

Time	✓	

FERMENTATION LOG

Date	Activity

Beer name:	

Beer Style:	

Brewer:	

Date brewed:	

Brewing method:	

Boil size	
Batch size	

Actual OG	
Actual FG	

Target OG	
Target FG	

Target ABV	
Actual ABV	

GRAINS

Name	Amount

HOPS / TOTAL IBU

Name	Amount	Time	IBU

YEAST

Name	
Type	
Style	

OTHER ADDITIONS

MASH AND SPARGE SCHEDULE

Time	Temp	✓	

BOIL SCHEDULE

Time	✓	

FERMENTATION LOG

Date	Activity

Beer name:

Beer Style:

Brewer:

Date brewed:

Brewing method:

Boil size	
Batch size	

Actual OG	
Actual FG	

Target OG	
Target FG	

Target ABV	
Actual ABV	

GRAINS	
Name	Amount

HOPS		TOTAL IBU	
Name	Amount	Time	IBU

YEAST	
Name	
Type	
Style	

OTHER ADDITIONS	

MASH AND SPARGE SCHEDULE

Time	Temp	✓	

BOIL SCHEDULE

Time	✓	

FERMENTATION LOG

Date	Activity

Beer name:	

Beer Style:	

Brewer:	

Date brewed:	

Brewing method:	

Boil size	
Batch size	

Target OG	
Target FG	

Actual OG	
Actual FG	

Target ABV	
Actual ABV	

GRAINS			HOPS		TOTAL IBU	
Name	Amount		Name	Amount	Time	IBU

YEAST	
Name	
Type	
Style	

OTHER ADDITIONS	

MASH AND SPARGE SCHEDULE

Time	Temp	✓	

BOIL SCHEDULE

Time	✓	

FERMENTATION LOG

Date	Activity

Beer name:	

Beer Style:	

Brewer:	

Date brewed:	

Brewing method:	

Boil size	
Batch size	

Target OG	
Target FG	

Actual OG	
Actual FG	

Target ABV	
Actual ABV	

GRAINS		HOPS		TOTAL IBU	
Name	Amount	Name	Amount	Time	IBU

YEAST	
Name	
Type	
Style	

OTHER ADDITIONS	

MASH AND SPARGE SCHEDULE

Time	Temp	✓	

BOIL SCHEDULE

Time	✓	

FERMENTATION LOG

Date	Activity

Beer name:

Beer Style:

Brewer:

Date brewed:

Brewing method:

Boil size	
Batch size	

Target OG	
Target FG	

Actual OG	
Actual FG	

Target ABV	
Actual ABV	

GRAINS	
Name	Amount

HOPS		TOTAL IBU	
Name	Amount	Time	IBU

YEAST	
Name	
Type	
Style	

OTHER ADDITIONS	

MASH AND SPARGE SCHEDULE

Time	Temp	✓	

BOIL SCHEDULE

Time	✓	

FERMENTATION LOG

Date	Activity

Beer name:

Beer Style:

Brewer:

Date brewed:

Brewing method:

Boil size	
Batch size	

Target OG	
Target FG	

Actual OG	
Actual FG	

Target ABV	
Actual ABV	

GRAINS		HOPS		TOTAL IBU	
Name	Amount	Name	Amount	Time	IBU

YEAST		OTHER ADDITIONS	
Name			
Type			
Style			

MASH AND SPARGE SCHEDULE

Time	Temp	✓	

BOIL SCHEDULE

Time	✓	

FERMENTATION LOG

Date	Activity

Beer name:

Beer Style:

Brewer:

Date brewed:

Brewing method:

Boil size	
Batch size	

Target OG	
Target FG	

Actual OG	
Actual FG	

Target ABV	
Actual ABV	

GRAINS	
Name	Amount

HOPS		TOTAL IBU	
Name	Amount	Time	IBU

YEAST	
Name	
Type	
Style	

OTHER ADDITIONS	

MASH AND SPARGE SCHEDULE

Time	Temp	✓	

BOIL SCHEDULE

Time	✓	

FERMENTATION LOG

Date	Activity

Beer name:

Beer Style:

Brewer:

Date brewed:

Brewing method:

Boil size	
Batch size	

Target OG	
Target FG	

Actual OG	
Actual FG	

Target ABV	
Actual ABV	

GRAINS		HOPS		TOTAL IBU	
Name	Amount	Name	Amount	Time	IBU

YEAST		OTHER ADDITIONS	
Name			
Type			
Style			

MASH AND SPARGE SCHEDULE

Time	Temp	✓	

BOIL SCHEDULE

Time	✓	

FERMENTATION LOG

Date	Activity

Beer name:

Beer Style:

Brewer:

Date brewed:

Brewing method:

Boil size	
Batch size	

Target OG	
Target FG	

Actual OG	
Actual FG	

Target ABV	
Actual ABV	

GRAINS	
Name	Amount

HOPS		TOTAL IBU	
Name	Amount	Time	IBU

YEAST	
Name	
Type	
Style	

OTHER ADDITIONS	

MASH AND SPARGE SCHEDULE

Time	Temp	✓	

BOIL SCHEDULE

Time	✓	

FERMENTATION LOG

Date	Activity

Beer name:

Beer Style:

Brewer:

Date brewed:

Brewing method:

Boil size	
Batch size	

Target OG	
Target FG	

Actual OG	
Actual FG	

Target ABV	
Actual ABV	

GRAINS		HOPS		TOTAL IBU	
Name	Amount	Name	Amount	Time	IBU

YEAST		OTHER ADDITIONS	
Name			
Type			
Style			

MASH AND SPARGE SCHEDULE

Time	Temp	✓	

BOIL SCHEDULE

Time	✓	

FERMENTATION LOG

Date	Activity

Beer name:

Beer Style:

Brewer:

Date brewed:

Brewing method:

Boil size		Target OG	
Batch size		Target FG	

Actual OG		Target ABV	
Actual FG		Actual ABV	

GRAINS		HOPS		TOTAL IBU	
Name	Amount	Name	Amount	Time	IBU

YEAST		OTHER ADDITIONS	
Name			
Type			
Style			

MASH AND SPARGE SCHEDULE

Time	Temp	✓	

BOIL SCHEDULE

Time	✓	

FERMENTATION LOG

Date	Activity

Beer name:

Beer Style:

Brewer:

Date brewed:

Brewing method:

Boil size	
Batch size	

Target OG	
Target FG	

Actual OG	
Actual FG	

Target ABV	
Actual ABV	

GRAINS			HOPS		TOTAL IBU	
Name	Amount		Name	Amount	Time	IBU

YEAST	
Name	
Type	
Style	

OTHER ADDITIONS	

MASH AND SPARGE SCHEDULE

Time	Temp	✓	

BOIL SCHEDULE

Time	✓	

FERMENTATION LOG

Date	Activity

Beer name:

Beer Style:

Brewer:

Date brewed:

Brewing method:

Boil size	
Batch size	

Target OG	
Target FG	

Actual OG	
Actual FG	

Target ABV	
Actual ABV	

GRAINS		HOPS		TOTAL IBU	
Name	Amount	Name	Amount	Time	IBU

YEAST	
Name	
Type	
Style	

OTHER ADDITIONS	

MASH AND SPARGE SCHEDULE

Time	Temp	✓	

BOIL SCHEDULE

Time	✓	

FERMENTATION LOG

Date	Activity

Beer name:

Beer Style:

Brewer:

Date brewed:

Brewing method:

Boil size	
Batch size	

Target OG	
Target FG	

Actual OG	
Actual FG	

Target ABV	
Actual ABV	

GRAINS

Name	Amount

HOPS / TOTAL IBU

Name	Amount	Time	IBU

YEAST

Name	
Type	
Style	

OTHER ADDITIONS

MASH AND SPARGE SCHEDULE

Time	Temp	✓	

BOIL SCHEDULE

Time	✓	

FERMENTATION LOG

Date	Activity

Beer name:

Beer Style:

Brewer:

Date brewed:

Brewing method:

Boil size	
Batch size	

Target OG	
Target FG	

Actual OG	
Actual FG	

Target ABV	
Actual ABV	

GRAINS		HOPS		TOTAL IBU	
Name	Amount	Name	Amount	Time	IBU

YEAST	
Name	
Type	
Style	

OTHER ADDITIONS	

MASH AND SPARGE SCHEDULE

Time	Temp	✓	

BOIL SCHEDULE

Time	✓	

FERMENTATION LOG

Date	Activity

Beer name:

Beer Style:

Brewer:

Date brewed:

Brewing method:

Boil size	
Batch size	

Target OG	
Target FG	

Actual OG	
Actual FG	

Target ABV	
Actual ABV	

GRAINS	
Name	Amount

HOPS		TOTAL IBU	
Name	Amount	Time	IBU

YEAST	
Name	
Type	
Style	

OTHER ADDITIONS	

MASH AND SPARGE SCHEDULE

Time	Temp	✓	

BOIL SCHEDULE

Time	✓	

FERMENTATION LOG

Date	Activity

Beer name:	

Beer Style:	

Brewer:	

Date brewed:	

Brewing method:	

Boil size		Target OG	
Batch size		Target FG	

Actual OG		Target ABV	
Actual FG		Actual ABV	

GRAINS		HOPS		TOTAL IBU	
Name	Amount	Name	Amount	Time	IBU

YEAST		OTHER ADDITIONS	
Name			
Type			
Style			

MASH AND SPARGE SCHEDULE

Time	Temp	✓	

BOIL SCHEDULE

Time	✓	

FERMENTATION LOG

Date	Activity

Beer name:

Beer Style:

Brewer:

Date brewed:

Brewing method:

Boil size	
Batch size	

Actual OG	
Actual FG	

Target OG	
Target FG	

Target ABV	
Actual ABV	

GRAINS	
Name	Amount

HOPS		TOTAL IBU	
Name	Amount	Time	IBU

YEAST	
Name	
Type	
Style	

OTHER ADDITIONS	

MASH AND SPARGE SCHEDULE

Time	Temp	✓	

BOIL SCHEDULE

Time	✓	

FERMENTATION LOG

Date	Activity

Beer name:

Beer Style:

Brewer:

Date brewed:

Brewing method:

Boil size	
Batch size	

Target OG	
Target FG	

Actual OG	
Actual FG	

Target ABV	
Actual ABV	

GRAINS			HOPS		TOTAL IBU	
Name	Amount		Name	Amount	Time	IBU

YEAST	
Name	
Type	
Style	

OTHER ADDITIONS	

MASH AND SPARGE SCHEDULE

Time	Temp	✓	

BOIL SCHEDULE

Time	✓	

FERMENTATION LOG

Date	Activity

Beer name:

Beer Style:

Brewer:

Date brewed:

Brewing method:

Boil size	
Batch size	

Target OG	
Target FG	

Actual OG	
Actual FG	

Target ABV	
Actual ABV	

GRAINS	
Name	Amount

HOPS		TOTAL IBU	
Name	Amount	Time	IBU

YEAST	
Name	
Type	
Style	

OTHER ADDITIONS	

MASH AND SPARGE SCHEDULE

Time	Temp	✓	

BOIL SCHEDULE

Time	✓	

FERMENTATION LOG

Date	Activity

Beer name:

Beer Style:

Brewer:

Date brewed:

Brewing method:

Boil size	
Batch size	

Target OG	
Target FG	

Actual OG	
Actual FG	

Target ABV	
Actual ABV	

GRAINS

Name	Amount

HOPS | | TOTAL IBU | |

Name	Amount	Time	IBU

YEAST

Name	
Type	
Style	

OTHER ADDITIONS

MASH AND SPARGE SCHEDULE

Time	Temp	✓	

BOIL SCHEDULE

Time	✓	

FERMENTATION LOG

Date	Activity

Beer name:

Beer Style:

Brewer:

Date brewed:

Brewing method:

Boil size	
Batch size	

Target OG	
Target FG	

Actual OG	
Actual FG	

Target ABV	
Actual ABV	

GRAINS			HOPS		TOTAL IBU	
Name	Amount		Name	Amount	Time	IBU

YEAST	
Name	
Type	
Style	

OTHER ADDITIONS	

MASH AND SPARGE SCHEDULE

Time	Temp	✓	

BOIL SCHEDULE

Time	✓	

FERMENTATION LOG

Date	Activity

Beer name:

Beer Style:

Brewer:

Date brewed:

Brewing method:

Boil size	
Batch size	

Target OG	
Target FG	

Actual OG	
Actual FG	

Target ABV	
Actual ABV	

GRAINS	
Name	Amount

HOPS		TOTAL IBU	
Name	Amount	Time	IBU

YEAST	
Name	
Type	
Style	

OTHER ADDITIONS	

MASH AND SPARGE SCHEDULE

Time	Temp	✓	

BOIL SCHEDULE

Time	✓	

FERMENTATION LOG

Date	Activity

Beer name:	

Beer Style:	

Brewer:	

Date brewed:	

Brewing method:	

Boil size	
Batch size	

Actual OG	
Actual FG	

Target OG	
Target FG	

Target ABV	
Actual ABV	

GRAINS		HOPS		TOTAL IBU	
Name	Amount	Name	Amount	Time	IBU

YEAST	
Name	
Type	
Style	

OTHER ADDITIONS	

MASH AND SPARGE SCHEDULE

Time	Temp	✓	

BOIL SCHEDULE

Time	✓	

FERMENTATION LOG

Date	Activity

Beer name:

Beer Style:

Brewer:

Date brewed:

Brewing method:

Boil size	
Batch size	

Target OG	
Target FG	

Actual OG	
Actual FG	

Target ABV	
Actual ABV	

GRAINS	
Name	Amount

HOPS		TOTAL IBU	
Name	Amount	Time	IBU

YEAST	
Name	
Type	
Style	

OTHER ADDITIONS	

MASH AND SPARGE SCHEDULE

Time	Temp	✓	

BOIL SCHEDULE

Time	✓	

FERMENTATION LOG

Date	Activity

Beer name:

Beer Style:

Brewer:

Date brewed:

Brewing method:

Boil size	
Batch size	

Target OG	
Target FG	

Actual OG	
Actual FG	

Target ABV	
Actual ABV	

GRAINS	
Name	Amount

HOPS		TOTAL IBU	
Name	Amount	Time	IBU

YEAST	
Name	
Type	
Style	

OTHER ADDITIONS	

MASH AND SPARGE SCHEDULE

Time	Temp	✓	

BOIL SCHEDULE

Time	✓	

FERMENTATION LOG

Date	Activity

Beer name:

Beer Style:

Brewer:

Date brewed:

Brewing method:

Boil size	
Batch size	

Target OG	
Target FG	

Actual OG	
Actual FG	

Target ABV	
Actual ABV	

GRAINS

Name	Amount

HOPS | TOTAL IBU

Name	Amount	Time	IBU

YEAST

Name	
Type	
Style	

OTHER ADDITIONS

MASH AND SPARGE SCHEDULE

Time	Temp	✓	

BOIL SCHEDULE

Time	✓	

FERMENTATION LOG

Date	Activity

Beer name:

Beer Style:

Brewer:

Date brewed:

Brewing method:

Boil size	
Batch size	

Target OG	
Target FG	

Actual OG	
Actual FG	

Target ABV	
Actual ABV	

GRAINS		
Name	Amount

HOPS		TOTAL IBU	
Name	Amount	Time	IBU

YEAST	
Name	
Type	
Style	

OTHER ADDITIONS	

MASH AND SPARGE SCHEDULE

Time	Temp	✓	

BOIL SCHEDULE

Time	✓	

FERMENTATION LOG

Date	Activity

We hope you enjoy our book.

Thank you!

Your feedback is very important to us. If you have encountered any issue with your coloring book, such as printing errors, faulty binding, paper bleeding or any other issue, please do not hesitate to contact me at:

ampergproducts@gmail.com

CPSIA information can be obtained
at www.ICGtesting.com
Printed in the USA
LVHW050317090221
678790LV00002B/127

9 784314 849593